# More Than What You See

Judi McDonald

BookLeaf Publishing

India | USA | UK

Presentation by *BookLeaf Publishing*

Web: www.bookleafpub.com

E-mail: info@bookleafpub.com

ISBN:9789358318630

First edition 2023

# PREFACE

Everyone is more than what you see, we are all a
bundle of emotions, thoughts and experiences.
And we all need to celebrate our inner self.

# More than what you see...

I am more than what you see.

I am all I wish to be.

I am resilience in the face of pain.

I am laughter caught in the rain.

I am my childhood in adult form.

I am hope in the face of a storm.

I am my future and I am my past.

I am all I am and I am vast.

# A Haiku of Peace

Floating alone in the cool and gentle ocean

Water laps along my skin

My mind drifts with the warm breeze and I am
at peace.

# Who Decided...

Who decided the sky was blue?
That rain was wet,
And You shouldn't go out in it.
Who decided that only young children should
jump in puddles.

Who decided that it is desirable to be young?
That age is an affliction
that we need to do everything we can to stave
off.
Who decided that wrinkles and grey hair are not
attractive.

Who decided that as the daughter becomes the
mother,
becomes the crone.
That she loses her beauty and value.
Who decided what old was.

Who decided that long legs were sexy.
That short girls were cute
And all must be as slim as possible.
Who decided what weight was beautiful.

Who decided that make up makes you look
better.
That to be beautiful you Should hide
what they say are your flaws.
Who decided being unique was wrong.

Who decided that you need to do it all.
Mother, wife, father, husband
Who decided how to define a human's value.

Who decided you shouldn't laugh loudly
That you should only sing
if others approve of your voice
Who decided you can only dance on the
dancefloor.

Who decided lawyers were worth more than
garbagemen.
That what you earn is how you define your
success.
Who decided that money equals respect.

Who decided that young, slim and rich were the
attractive ideal.
That you must conform to be acceptable.
Who decided that being different was
undesirable.

Who decides that you are too old.

too big, too small, too loud, too different, too
much.
Who decides that it's not enough to just be you.

# Promises

I stand on the edge
The darkness calls
Wooing me sweetly
With promises of apathy

It would be so easy to fall
down
down
down
Into the darkness below
with its promise of oblivion

I force myself to turn away
put my back to that sweet abyss
I move forward
towards the promise of another day.

# The Hug

Arms,
wrapped tight around my body
firm in their hold.

Warmth flows from deep inside me
my arms encase them
hold a little tighter.

Contentment, Love, Warmth, strength,
feelings spread through my existence
seeping into my soul
I close my eyes
I don't want to let go

Separating slowly
Hands lingering, petting,
The feelings stay
The warmth turns to a glow
I can breathe a little longer.

# I'm Fine

I smile
I say I'm Fine
Because that is what you need to hear
But inside the tears build behind my eyes

I smile
I say I'm Fine
Coz you need to think I am okay
But inside my broken pieces rub together like
shattered bones

I smile
I say I'm Fine
Coz i can't let the mask slip
But inside I am screaming for help.

I smile
I say I'm Fine
Because only one of us can be broken at a time.

# Dance

The drum reverberates
echoing in my bones
my pulse copies the rhythm.

Bodies sway pressed together
Strangers become one with the music
My eyes close

Arms move to the melody
raise, lower, swing, sway
my head falls back as I move

Feet shuffle, step, stomp, tap
moving together in time
Euphoria fills my mind.

Hands clap, voices sing,
Bodies jump, jive, spin,
time becomes meaningless

The music fades,
The lights become brighter
we are all separate strangers again.

I am spent and filled with joy.

# Resilience

I take a breath
I take a chance
I strive and I hope
And I Pray

Only to hear nothing
Get no reply
Rejection, Failure
On replay

It sinks in under my skin
I wonder what's wrong with me
Why they don't want me to stay

But I stand up, head high
and look yet again
the next might be the one
Resilience wins today.

# Sated

The waiting
The wanting
The heat runs through my body

A soft touch
A caress
Teasing along my skin

A gasp
A sigh
The need building more

A firmer grip
I take control
Mouth dry with desire

I wet my lips
I slake my thirst
I am sated

For now.

# What is she?

Is she a beauty
Shining so bright
You can only compare her
To the stars at night

Is she a wonder
Amazing and true
That you can't imagine
the pain she goes through

Is she a warrior
So tough and so strong
That hold it all together
That fights all thats wrong

Is she an angel
So sweet and so kind
She is so gentle
You swear she is divine

Is she a goddess
So fierce and powerful
Also grace and mercy
From deep within her soul

Or is she a woman
A mix of all above
But most of all a Woman is
A person full of love.

# Touch

Why would you think the touch is wrong?
Touch is the most soft communication of all.
Never forget the comfort and humanity of a
touch.

All that is touch is not want,
Need, by all account is emotional.
Are you upset by how soulful it is?
Does it tear you apart to see a touch so
temperamental?

When I think of touch, I see a delicious secret.
Never forget the erotic and sensuality of a touch.
A gentle touch, a light tickle along the skin.

Touch can be an adventure.
A grand escapade of touch.
Long strokes, a pinch, a grope
Never forget the crafty and tricky adventure.

We can communicate by touch
A hand shake, a pat on the back
A slap, a punch, a hard shove

But touch can be forgiveness as well

A touch can lead to salvation
A touch can save a life.

# Serotonin boosters

The warmth of the sun
kissing my bare skin
on a sunny spring day

Digging my toes into the warm sand
and feeling the sand slide away
as I lift them up again

The sound of waves
breaking against the shore
as I watch the ebb and flow

Laying back to look at the sky
finding shapes in the clouds
floating in the vast blue

The crackle of a fire
on a cold night
whilst drinking hot chocolate

A puppy,
fat belly jiggling
tail wagging
as it wriggles in my arms.

The smell of dew
coming from the grass
in the evening of a summer day.

The sound of rain
on a tin roof
when your warm inside

The purr of a cat
asleep on your lap
as you pet the softness of their fur.

Laughing with people
until your tummy hurts
and you can't stop smiling.

The feel of a hug
that tight strong one
that doesn't want to end.

# Primrose's revenge

A poem, A prose,
About sweet Primrose
Who everyone thought was so cute.

And a terrible boy,
Whose name was Elroy,
Who decide Primrose would suit.

With flowers and sweets
and other special treats,
Elroy wooed Prim to wed.

Agreeing to be MRS,
She got swept up in kisses,
And Elroy took her to bed.

Things then went sour,
When within the hour,
Of awakening the very next day.

Elroy quickly departed,
leaving Prim brokenhearted,
saying he realized he was gay.

Yet just a week later,
Elroy, the gator,
was seen with a girl new.

Primrose's anger,
arose in a clangor,
she swore to see him blue.

Prim took to work,
she knew such a jerk,
would have done this plenty before.

And she found each lady,
Elroy had dealt shady,
they agreed to what Prim had in store.

It came to the day,
In a little cafe,
Elroy took his faux bride.

There they all were,
His girls from before,
sitting there all side by side.

Elroy looked round,
and nearly fell down,
as they stood all as one.

They had plotted and planned,
To leave him unmanned,
and show him what he had done.

With pretend pregnant bellies,
his exes did rally,
to show him his erroneous ways

Elroy fled to the hills,
where he lives stills,
celibate to the end of his days.

# alone

The crowd
pushes
brushes
shoves
bumps

people crushed together all moving in different
directions rush rush rush

I stand still
alone

# Does death like its job?

I like my job
I help people
people who are hurting
who are tired
who are ready
to move into the next step

I hate my job
I take from others
I hurt them
I take their love
their light
their reason for living

I want to tell those people
that it is ok
that it was time
that those I helped were ready

but those I hurt will not see
they are blinded by grief

# Anxiety Unbound

I am jittering apart
The jagged edges of the world
sticking
  jabbing
    sharp
into my soft being.

I am an electric current
with no purpose
no place to go.

I am skittering along
the edge
the edge
the edge
of everything

I am to big for my home,
it is too small to contain me
but
the world is too big
and I am lost

I want to scream
cry

        rant
            rave
about everything
about nothing

I am empty

I am my anxiety
unbound.

# Signs

I asked the universe
for a sign
Will riches
ever be mine

In return
it gave me
a shoe.

I asked the universe
for a sign
will fame ever be mine

In return
it gave me
no clue

I asked the universe
for a sign
will happiness
ever be mine

In return
it gave me
you.

# Diazepam

Softly floating

A fluffy cloud
    above the wordly worries

My anxiety falls away

I am cushioned
    from the harsh reality

I drift

I float

I am serenity
  and I am calm

I can finally sleep.

# Sweet memories

A touch

A sweet caress

Fingertips softly skimming skin

I close my eyes

A tear falls

Memories of your touch

I turn

you are gone

forever.

# Who's Fault

Father punishes me
with a grounding, a smack, a belt
He says why don't I listen
Why don't I do what I am told

It's all my fault.

Mother says she never wanted me
She didn't want more kids
Why did I have to come along
I made her fat and unhappy

It's all my fault.

Brother says to stay away
His friend wants to do things to me
That I need to hide myself
Not show myself when they are around.

It's all my fault.

Sister says she hates me
She wants to go have fun
Not babysit me all the time
I ruin everything

It's all my fault.

Teacher says I need to try more
to act more like the other kids
Try to fit in with them
That then they will stop bullying me

It's all my fault.


My date takes advantage of me
He said he couldn't stop himself.
I was too beautiful
I made him too excited.

It's all my fault.


Maybe the world would be better
If I was not in it.
Then people wouldn't do the
things I make them do.

Since it's all my fault.

# The power within

In the storm of life, we find our way,
Through trials and troubles, come what may.
With a heart that's fierce and a spirit untamed,
We stand tall, broken but unashamed.

Inner strength, a fire deep inside,
A force that can't be easily denied.
It's the spark that fuels our inner fight,
To push through the darkness and reach for the
light.

When life's troubles weigh heavy on our chest,
We rise with courage, we do our best.
Resilience, the ability to start anew,
No matter how tough, no matter how blue.

In the face of adversity, we find our grace,
With unwavering spirit, we set our pace.
For in our hearts, the power resides,
To weather the storms, to reach the tides.

With inner strength as our trusted friend,
We'll endure, we'll survive, and we'll mend.
With each challenge we face, we'll only grow,

Our resilience will shine, and our spirits will glow.